Devon

BRADWELL
BOOKS

A TASTE OF DEVON

SALCOMBE · ODDICOMBE · COMBE MARTIN · PLYMOUTH HOE

Introduction

Step inside Bradwell's Images of Devon and treat yourself to an enchanting visual feast. Using outstanding technical skills coupled with an absolute love of their subject matter, Susan and Andrew Caffrey have created a collection of images that portray the essence of Devon in all its depth and variety. From the iconic to the unknown, these photographs will have you itching to return and explore again and again, and perhaps give you some ideas for capturing your own photographs!

Enjoy!

Teignmouth

On the north bank of the River Teign lies Teignmouth, a bustling harbour and traditional English holiday resort. Teignmouth has something for everyone; from soft, sandy beaches to the grand Victorian pier and fascinating architecture; or take the Teignmouth to Dawlish railway walk for glorious views of the English Riviera.

Torquay

Famous for its sandstone cliffs, clear blue waters and swaying palms, Torquay attracts surfers and tourists year after year. Soak up the Mediterranean atmosphere with a stroll along the pier, relax on idyllic white beaches, or take in spectacular sea views from one of the harbour's waterside restaurants.

Salcombe

Salcombe's balmy weather and stunning scenery make this historic fishing port a popular retreat. Brimming with West Country charm, the vibrant town offers bars and restaurants serving the best in Devon produce. Ferry trips run to hidden-away beaches and coves, where visitors can enjoy bathing and a variety of water sports.

Postbridge

Postbridge lies at the heart of Dartmoor, and makes the perfect gateway to the north moor for walkers. The 12th-century 'clapper bridge', from which the hamlet takes its name, is a must-see. Drop in to the Village Store across the road and complete your visit with a traditional Devon cream tea.

Widecombe in-the-Moor

Nestled in the valley of the East Webburn River, Widecombe-in-the-Moor is known for its village green, where wild ponies and cattle can often be spotted grazing.

Wander the ancient tracks around the village and up Widecombe Hill for spectacular views of the valley, and stop at one of many delightful inns for a meal and a drink.

Plymouth Hoe

Plymouth Hoe looks out over Plymouth Sound, one of the world's most beautiful natural harbours. Climb to the top of the iconic Smeaton's Tower lighthouse for a truly stunning view. Along the coastline, you'll find ice cream stands and cafés which make great spots for watching the boats come and go.

Brixham

The small fishing town of Brixham is home to award-winning beaches, cosy country pubs and pretty fishermen's cottages. Visitors can enjoy boating and diving, take a guided tour of the world-famous Old Fish Market, and explore the glorious scenery with walks along the coast or through the surrounding woodland.

Anstey's Cove

Between Torquay and Babbacombe sits the peaceful shingle beach of Anstey's Cove. It's the perfect place to rent a deckchair, paddle in the sea, or enjoy refreshments at the beach café. Venture into the wooded hillside and walk the coastal path, discovering wildlife and rare plants along the way.

Lynmouth

The picturesque town of Lynmouth is found along Devon's North Coast, within Exmoor National Park. Here you'll find historic houses, beautiful gardens, red deer and wild Exmoor ponies. Lynmouth is famed for its high sea cliffs, best viewed from a ride on the Cliff Railway, which runs up to Lynton.

NEXT BOAT TRIP SAILS:
FROM: HARBOUR SLIPWAY OR LOW TIDE LANDINGS

NEXT EXMOOR BOAT TRIP: 2 PM TODAY
THE BEST WAY TO SEE THE COAST
EACH TRIP PASSES A SELECTION OF THESE PLACES

VALLEY of ROCKS

LEE ABBEY

WOODY BAY

HEDDON'S MOUTH

OPEN ONLY ONE TRIP PER DAY

1 HOUR TRIP TO WOODY BAY

CAPACITY TODAY: 12/30 PASSENGERS
MINIMUM 6 REQUIRED TO SAIL

PLEASE TAKE A LEAFLET!

BOOK (Here) On Boat
1 HOUR BOAT TRIP TO WOODY BAY
NEXT TRIP TODAY 2 PM
£10 Per Person

OR WHY NOT TRY
1 HOUR DRIFT FISHING
NEXT TRIP: 3 PM SAT
£10 PER PERSON
EARLY BOOKING ADVISED

•KEEP YOUR CATCH! –BRING A BAG
•ALL RODS AND GEAR SUPPLIED
•CHILDREN AND NOVICES WELCOME

Paignton

The beaches of Paignton offer water-skiing, boat trips, or simply a place to relax in the sun. Head to Paignton Pier for traditional seaside fun, from amusement arcades to crazy golf. A trip on the Dartmouth Steam Railway is the ideal way to take in some of the UK's most beautiful coastline.

Dartmoor

From rugged moors to ancient woodland to stately granite tors, Dartmoor offers some of England's most impressive and varied landscapes. Walk or cycle your way across open spaces or along the many gentle trails. Swim in clear rivers and enjoy a picnic on the beautiful rocky beaches that line the banks.

Dartmouth

Dartmouth in South Devon lies at the mouth of the River Dart, making it perfect for fishing trips, exploring the creeks, and boat trips to nearby towns or to Dartmouth Castle. Visit in August and experience the town's famous regatta, with crabbing, boat parades and a world-class air show.

A TASTE OF DEVON

BAGGY POINT · ODDICOMBE · DARTMOUTH · COMBE MARTIN